Union Public Library

Judy Baca

by Mary Olmstead

Chicago, Illinois

Union Public Library

© 2005 Raintree
Published by Raintree, a division of Reed Elsevier, Inc.
Chicago, Illinois
Customer Service: 888-363-4266
Visit our website at www.raintreelibrary.com

All rights reserved. No part of this book may be reproduced
or transmitted in any form or by any means, electronic
or mechanical, including photocopying, recording,
taping, or any information storage and retrieval system,
without permission in writing from the publisher.

For information, address the publisher
Raintree, 100 N. LaSalle, Suite 1200, Chicago, IL 60602

Photo research by Scott Braut
Printed and bound in China by South China Printing
Co. Ltd.

09 08 07 06 05
10 9 8 7 6 5 4 3 2 1

Library of Congress Cataloging-in-Publication Data
Judy Baca / Mary Olmstead.
    p. cm. -- (Hispanic-American biographies)
Includes bibliographical references and index.
  ISBN 1-4109-0709-0 (lib. bdg.-hardcover) -- ISBN 1-
4109-0915-8 (pbk.)
  1. Baca, Judith Francisca--Juvenile literature. 2.
Hispanic American
painters--California--Biography--Juvenile literature. [1.
Baca, Judith
Francisca. 2. Artists. 3. Mexican Americans--Biography.
4.
Women--Biography.] I. Title. II. Series: Olmstead, Mary.
Hispanic-American biographies.
  ND237.B13O44 2004
  759.13--dc22
                                        2003024764

JB
BACA, J
c. 1

Acknowledgments
The publisher would like to thank the following for
permission to reproduce photographs:
pp. 4, 10, 11, 14, 27, 46, 48, 57 SPARC; p. 6 "The Great
Wall of Los Angeles, Pre-Historic California" Acrylic on
cast concrete. 1976/SPARC; pp. 8, 23 Bettmann/Corbis;
p. 16 California State University, Northridge; p. 18
"Cactus Heart" Oil stick on paper. 23" x 29", 1980.
From the collection of Armando Duron/SPARC; p. 24
Stephanie Maze/Corbis; p. 30 "The Great Wall of Los
Angeles, Uprising of the Mujeres" 8' x 24'. Acrylic on
wood, 1979/SPARC; p. 32 Corbis; p. 37 Rivera, Diego
(1866-1957) © Banco de Mexico Trust, Fin del Corrido,
detail of "Children Learning". Mural, Court of Fiestas,
Corridor of the Agrarian Revolution, West Wall, c.1922-
28. Secretaria de Educacion Publica, Mexico
City/D.F.Schalkwijk/Art Resource, NY; p. 38 "The Great
Wall of Los Angeles, Charlie Parker and Billy Holiday at
the Dunbar Hotel", from the 1930's section/SPARC; p.
40 "The Great Wall of Los Angeles, Fighting 442nd"
from the 1940's section. 1982/SPARC; p. 42 "Triumph of
the Hearts," part of the "World Wall: A Vision of the
Future Without Fear." 1990/SPARC; p. 43 The Mexican
panel from the "World Wall: A Vision of the Future
without Fear, Tlazolteotl: Fuerza Creadora de lo No
Tejido" (Creatice Force of the Un-Woven). 10' x 30',
Acrylic on canvas. 1999/SPARC; p. 54 Damian
Dovarganes/AP Wide World Photo; p. 59 "La Memoria
de Nuestra Tierra: Colorado" Denver International
Airport, Denver, Colorado. 10' x 50' digital mural,
2000/SPARC

Cover photograph by SPARC

Every effort has been made to contact copyright holders
of any material reproduced in this book. Any omissions
will be rectified in subsequent printings if notice is given
to the publisher.

Some words are shown in bold,
like this. You can find out
what they mean by looking in
the glossary.

Contents

Judy Baca is a mural artist who is known for her work with young people. Judy developed mural art programs for the city of Los Angeles because she wanted to help people in her community.

Introduction

Judy Baca is an artist and an art teacher. She is known around the world for her work. Her colorful murals have brought history to life. A mural is a large painting that is done on walls or other large surfaces. Judy's murals express the hopes, dreams, and opinions of many people. Her murals have shown how people think and feel.

Judy has made a difference in the lives of many people by using art to teach peace and understanding. In one case, she worked with gang members. Gangs are groups acting together, sometimes against the law. Judy hired many kids who had gotten in trouble at school or with the law. She gave them direction and helped them set goals. They painted murals in the neighborhoods of East Los Angeles.

The colorful murals show scenes from the lives of people from the neighborhood. The murals let their voices be heard. People were impressed with Judy's work. She had succeeded in getting gang members to stop fighting and helped them paint something

This section of The Great Wall of Los Angeles *shows a saber-toothed tiger and other animals from prehistoric times.*

pleasing. Judy's work spread. She directed a mural program for all of Los Angeles that became very popular. Judy saw how art could help shape a more peaceful world. She wanted to spread her work to as many people as she could.

Judy had ideas for creating art with groups of people. She helped start a center for mural art called the Social and Public Art Resource Center (SPARC). Through SPARC, more people got involved in painting murals. SPARC's first project was a mural called *The Great Wall of Los Angeles*. It is the work Judy is most famous for and is thought to be the world's longest mural.

The Great Wall mural is 0.5 miles (0.8 kilometers) long. It shows the history of Los Angeles from **prehistoric** times through modern times. It shows the lives of the many **ethnic** groups who lived there. For some people it was the first time their stories had ever been told.

Judy changed the face of Los Angeles with her colorful murals. She convinced gang members that spreading peace through art was better than fighting. She helped them make a difference. In the process, she changed their hearts and their minds. Many people were grateful for those changes. They learned how to cooperate for a purpose. They learned how to create beautiful things.

In Her Own Words

"I am moved in the heart. I see an issue, something I can care about, and then I go about finding solutions in the way I can as an artist."

—Judy Baca

"I got the idea that making art was probably one of the most important human activities that anyone could engage in."

—Judy Baca

"I always had the feeling that art was the celebration of the senses. I want to make art that will ask people to use all of their senses."

—Judy Baca

This photo shows a busy street in Los Angeles in the early 1950s.

Chapter 1: Growing Up

Judith Francisca Baca was born on September 20, 1946, in Los Angeles, California. When she was very little, Judy lived in a house full of women. She lived with her mother, her aunts Rita and Delia, and her grandmother Francisca. Judy learned early in life that she was loved.

Judy's family lived in South Central Los Angeles in a Spanish-speaking neighborhood. At home, Judy's aunt Delia was a wonderful friend. Judy described her aunt as someone who was not "grown up in her head. It was like she was five, my age, only she was big." Aunt Delia always played with Judy.

Judy's Grandmother

Judy's father was a musician. She never knew him when she was growing up. Judy's mother Ortensia worked in a tire factory. Judy's grandmother Francisca took care of her while her mother

This photo of Judy as a young child was taken when she lived in South Central Los Angeles.

worked. She spoke only Spanish. Judy watched and learned from her. She was very religious, and she was also the neighborhood healer. A healer is a person who uses traditional beliefs and medicine to help sick people. Judy's grandmother used herbs, love, and prayer. She listened to people's troubles and comforted them. Judy saw that her grandmother was a healer of things related to the body and the heart. Judy wanted to be like her grandmother. Judy also later became a healer of the social problems of the community.

A New Life

In 1952, when she was six, Judy's life changed. Her mother married again and they moved to a suburb of Los Angeles called Pacoima. Later that year, Judy's half-brother Gary was born.

Judy was happy to have a new baby brother and a father, but she missed her old life. She missed her grandmother and her aunts. She missed the Spanish-speaking neighborhood she had lived in. She felt that way most when she was old enough to start school. In school, Judy experienced **discrimination.** Some people did not treat her fairly because she was Mexican American.

Judy was around eight years old when this photo was taken. Her mother Ortensia is holding Judy's baby brother Gary.

Judy was not allowed to speak Spanish at school. She recalled, "I remember being in rooms with people speaking this other language. I didn't understand the words, but I knew that they were saying I was less than they were because I didn't speak English."

At first, Judy struggled in school. She did not understand everything. But Judy had learned not to be afraid to speak up. Judy told herself she would learn English better. She was very outgoing. Every day, she learned a few more words.

A New Interest

Art became Judy's favorite subject and Judy's teacher encouraged her interest. She often allowed Judy to sit in a corner and paint by herself. Drawing and painting gave Judy a break from learning new words in English. Even at home, Judy often spent her free time drawing. She liked doing this almost more than anything.

Judy was an active child. She loved to swim and play outside with other children. She enjoyed playing with her little brother Gary. Judy was six years older, but she and Gary were close. When Judy was eleven, another child was born, her stepsister Diane.

Push to Succeed

Judy's grandparents were from Mexico. They settled in La Junta, Colorado, which was where Judy's mother grew up. After she moved to Los Angeles, Ortensia worked hard. She wanted Judy to have more choices than she did. That is why she made sure Judy did well in school. She knew a good education would help Judy.

After Judy's struggles with English were over, school became easier. She was smart. She earned good grades in all subjects. But art was the subject that she liked the most.

Being Mexican

The United States is a mix of many different **cultures.** There are things about every **ethnic** group that set it apart from others.

Curanderismo: Mexican Folk Medicine

The Spanish name for Mexican folk medicine is *curanderismo.* It comes from the Spanish word *curar,* which means "to heal." This folk tradition goes back five hundred years. It is a combination of Aztec, Native American, Spanish, and African medicine. *Curanderismo* lives on in Mexico and in those parts of the United States with a large Mexican-American population.

Some illnesses, such as the evil eye (*mal de ojo* in Spanish), are believed to be caused by evil spirits. The evil eye is cured by praying and rubbing the sick person with a chicken egg.

Other illnesses are thought to come from natural causes. They are often treated with herbs, such as *yerba buena* for stomachaches and aloe vera for burns. Treatment of minor illnesses like stomachache is usually done by the mother, grandmother, or aunt in a family.

It may be the language the group speaks. It may be the holidays the group celebrates. They may cook foods in a certain way or wear a certain style of clothing. Many people are proud of their ethnic backgrounds.

Most Americans were white when Judy was growing up. Many Mexican Americans tried hard to be like white people and to blend in more with them. They felt it was the way to begin to succeed in America. That was why Judy's mom wanted her to speak English well. Her mother believed it would make Judy's life easier.

After college, Judy became an art teacher at the high school she had attended, Bishop Alemany High School.

Chapter 2: Finding Her Way

Judy went to a private Catholic school called Bishop Alemany High School. Many of the teachers at the school were nuns. Nuns are women who give their lives to religious work in the Catholic Church. They spend their lives helping others. Judy worked hard in school to get good grades. She still loved to draw and paint more than any other activity.

Judy graduated from high school in 1964. She applied to California State University at Northridge. She wanted to study art. These were busy years for Judy. She studied and she worked to get money to pay for college.

During her first year in college, Judy fell in love. She got married when she was nineteen. Judy stayed in school after she married. She was not sure what to do with her life. Judy had been brought up to be independent. She had been taught to follow her own path. Now she was married.

Judy was not sure she wanted a traditional life. But she felt pressure from her family. They did not want her to be an artist because the chances for success as an artist usually are not good. Judy, though, finally decided that she had to be an artist.

Judy felt alone in college. Most of the students were white. She felt cut off from her **culture.** Judy missed hearing Spanish. She missed the everyday things from her earlier life. She missed the food and the music from her childhood.

This photograph shows the campus of California State University at Northridge where Judy went to college.

Studying Art

In spite of her feelings, Judy stayed in school. She earned a degree in art. She studied art history and took studio art classes. In studio art classes, students draw and paint. An experienced art teacher **supervises** their work.

Judy liked to paint in a modern style of art called **abstract** art. It is not an easy kind of art to understand. Abstract art uses colors and shapes to express emotions and ideas. It does not show objects exactly as they appear in nature. People cannot always tell what an abstract painting is supposed to be about.

Judy's grandmother looked at her granddaughter's paintings. She asked Judy, "What is this? What's it for?" In her world, everything had a purpose. Everything had a meaning. The purpose of Judy's art was not easy for her to understand.

Judy thought about her paintings. The purpose in her works of art was not always clear to others. It was not art that other people easily understood. Judy wanted her art to have meaning for her family and her community. She wanted to make art her grandmother would understand. Could she do it?

Judy decided to make a different sort of art. It would not be the kind of art found in art galleries. An art gallery is a place where art is displayed for people to see. Judy's family and the people she knew did not go to art galleries.

Judy decided to make art that connected to her Mexican-American background. She would paint pictures that showed her beliefs. She would use the bright colors of her **abstract** paintings. She would use the bold shapes. But her paintings would have everyday meanings.

Cactus Heart *is an example of the abstract art Judy has painted. Abstract art uses color and shape to express a feeling. It does not show objects as they actually appear in nature.*

A Return to High School

Judy graduated from college in 1969 with a degree in art. She was 23. She got a job as an art teacher at her old high school. In her classes were students from many **ethnic** backgrounds. They did not get along with each other sometimes.

Judy felt that they needed to learn to cooperate and she decided to have them paint a mural on a school wall. The school mural was Judy's first cooperative art project. A cooperative art project is one in which people work together to make art.

Judy saw how students were forced to cooperate with each other. If they did not, the mural could not be painted. Judy knew that students had learned a valuable lesson. They had learned to work with each other. She hoped they might cooperate better with people in other areas of their lives.

The mural project also helped Judy. It helped her find a good way to work with students. It helped her develop a method she would use many times in future projects.

Vietnam War

Vietnam is a country in Southeast Asia. France ruled there from the 1850s to 1954. After World War II ended in 1945, a Vietnamese man named Ho Chi Minh led a movement to make Vietnam independent. His soldiers fought until France left in 1954.

After the French left, the Vietnamese people disagreed on how to rule their country, so Vietnam was divided into North Vietnam and South Vietnam. North Vietnam had a **communist** government. The south had a **republican** government. The United States sent soldiers to stop communism from spreading to South Vietnam.

American soldiers stayed much longer than anyone planned, and their numbers grew. By 1965 over 150,000 United States soldiers were fighting the North Vietnamese. By 1968 more than half a million United States soldiers were in Vietnam. Many Vietnamese did not want the United States in their country. People in the United States also argued with each other about their country's part in the war. Thousands of Americans marched against the war.

In 1973 the United States withdrew from Vietnam without winning the war. Two years later, the war ended when the communists took over South Vietnam. More than one million Vietnamese and 58,000 Americans died in the Vietnam War.

El Movimiento

Judy did not keep her job at the high school very long. After work, she became involved in *El Movimiento,* Spanish for "The Movement." *El Movimiento* describes activities that took place during the mid-1960s and early 1970s. Thousands of people wanted to help those who had not been treated fairly by society. They made speeches and marched in the streets to get attention for their cause.

Some people worked for better treatment of African Americans or other **ethnic** groups. Some fought for equal treatment of women. A man named César Chávez led a movement to help Mexican-American farm workers. Farm workers wanted to be paid more. They wanted better treatment on the job.

Judy joined a part of *El Movimiento* called the peace movement. The United States was fighting in a country called Vietnam. Many people believed the United States should not fight in Vietnam's **civil war.** They did not think United States soldiers should be in Vietnam. Several teachers at Judy's school joined her. They took part in marches against the war.

There was a new principal at the school where Judy taught. The new principal thought that the teachers should not take part in peace marches. The teachers who marched against the war in Vietnam were fired. Judy lost her job. She worried. She was afraid no one would hire her to teach again.

César Chávez (1927–1993)

César Chávez is remembered by many as a great American hero. He worked to improve working conditions for migrant workers. Migrant workers are people who move from place to place to harvest crops. For many years they were not treated well.

Chávez was born in 1927 near Yuma, Arizona. In the 1930s, his family lost everything they owned. Afterward, he spent part of his childhood and early adult years as a migrant worker in California. He knew growers often cheated farm workers out of money. Most farm workers were very poor. They could not always feed their families.

In 1962 Chávez organized an agricultural labor **union.** A labor union is a group of workers who join together for a common purpose. Chávez was a peaceful man. He did not allow people who joined the farm workers' union to use violence against the growers, even when the growers used violence against them.

After several years Chávez helped farm workers win more money and better working conditions. People everywhere heard about their struggle and the man who led them to victory. Chávez had shown people that nonviolence could bring about peaceful changes in society. He said, "Once social change begins, it cannot be reversed." Many young people like Judy Baca took César Chávez's nonviolent beliefs to heart.

César Chávez was a labor leader who fought for fair treatment of farm workers. His belief in nonviolence influenced young people like Judy Baca to work peacefully for change in society during the 1960s and 1970s.

Boyle Heights is a Hispanic neighborhood in Los Angeles where Judy worked as an art teacher in the early 1970s. The painting on this wall showed the pride felt by the Mexican Americans who lived there.

Chapter 3:
Painting with Kids

Judy did not have to worry. She found another teaching job. The city of Los Angeles hired her to teach art in parks for a summer program. She taught young children and senior citizens. She worked in a neighborhood called Boyle Heights, a neighborhood that had many Mexican Americans. Boyle Heights also had the highest number of gangs in the United States.

Judy's job took her to different parks. She could move freely between the neighborhood parks, but teenage boys who were in gangs could not. Different gangs claimed territory in the neighborhood. There was fighting when more than one gang claimed the same territory. When a gang caught a different gang's member in their territory, there was trouble. Gangs fought to keep other gangs out of their territory.

Most of the teens spent their time hanging out on the street or in the parks. They painted **graffiti** on public walls. Graffiti marked the territory claimed by each gang. Judy knew that writing on public walls was a part of life in the *barrio*. People did not have much control over their neighborhood. Most people did not own their own homes. **Landlords** owned most of the buildings.

Painting graffiti made people feel like the neighborhood belonged to them. It made them feel that the buildings were a part of their community. Judy explained, "You could read a wall and learn everything you needed to know about that community." You could read both good and bad things. Graffiti told who lived in the neighborhood. It also told which gangs claimed that space.

The Art Lady

Graffiti divided Boyle Heights. Gangs used it to show their territory in the neighborhood. Judy wanted to find something to **unite** the neighborhood. She got an idea. She would teach art to gang members. That would give them something positive to do. Gang members got used to seeing Judy every day. Their shouts of "Hey, art lady!" became friendly. Soon some of them began to show Judy their drawings.

Judy thought about the mural she had made at Bishop Alemany High School. Her students had learned to cooperate. Judy thought painting murals could unite gang members in Boyle

Judy works with young people from different gangs in the Boyle Heights neighborhood. Judy is third from the left, crouching.

Heights, too. Murals were similar to graffiti in some ways. They both told stories. But murals told stories in a more positive way. A mural could tell the history of a place and its people. It could also show how people lived.

Many of the young men Judy got to know in the parks of Boyle Heights began to trust her. They were willing to listen. They wanted to learn. Judy told them she wanted to form a mural team to paint. Nobody knew what a mural was. Judy explained that they were going to paint a great big picture on a wall. They would meet after she got off work.

A Neighborhood Project

About twenty gang members were on Judy's mural team. They were between 16 and 21 years old. The team was called *Las Vistas Nuevas,* Spanish for "New Views." Judy hoped to teach the team a new view of life. She wanted them to have a different view of their neighborhood, too.

The members of *Las Vistas Nuevas* belonged to four different gangs. They were not used to getting along with each other. They were used to fighting. Judy told them they had to get along. They could not paint a mural if they could not cooperate with each other.

During the summer of 1970, *Las Vistas Nuevas* painted three murals. The murals showed **barrio** life. Their first mural was painted on the three-sided band shell of Hollenbeck Park. It was titled *Mi Abuelita,* Spanish for "My Grandmother." The mural showed the important position of grandmothers in Hispanic families. The mural reflected their Mexican roots and the values they believed in.

The mural team learned to respect and share public places. They learned that they could get along with people from other gangs. Working with gang members made Judy happy, too. She was not just painting. She was using art to bring people together.

Working Through Problems

Judy learned a lot that summer. She began to realize that everyone needs a purpose. Everyone needs to feel they belong somewhere. That is why different gangs competed to have their own space in the neighborhood.

Las Vistas Nuevas had a problem. Other gang members did not want the mural team in their territory. They tried to cause trouble for the artists. To protect themselves, Judy's group had some team members act as **lookouts.**

The lookouts whistled when someone approached who might cause trouble. The artists then climbed down quickly from the **scaffold** or platform they were working on. They would go inside the band shell through the stage doors. Then they would wait for an all-clear signal from the lookout.

The mural team faced another problem. The police did not support Judy's work because they did not think it was safe to have gangs working in the park. The police worried that they would fight, and people might get hurt. The police told Judy not to bring gangs to the park anymore. The police said they would arrest the team members.

One day Judy's group heard the lookout whistle. It was a special signal to let them know a plain-clothes police officer was

This section of The Great Wall of Los Angeles *is called* Uprising of the Mujeres (mujeres *is Spanish for "women").*

approaching. A plain-clothes officer is a police officer who wears regular clothes instead of a police uniform. Judy told her group to keep painting. She wondered what would happen. She hoped she could convince the police officer to let them keep working.

A Bit of Good Luck

"Judy Baca?" a man's voice called. Judy expected to see a police officer ready to arrest her mural team. Instead, she saw a man named Sy Greben. He was her boss at the Department of Recreation and Parks. He asked, "Are you being paid to do this work?"

Judy was afraid to answer. She did not have permission to be painting on city property. She was worried. What if Mr. Greben was there to tell her to stop painting? Judy gathered her courage. She said very politely, "No. I am an art teacher in your parks working on my own time."

Judy held her breath. She waited to hear what Mr. Greben would say next. He looked at the young art teacher. He looked at her crew. They all wore paint-covered clothes. Then he studied the mural they were working on. He saw how the group cooperated.

Sy Greben understood right away the importance and the power of Judy's work. The people were cooperating. If they cooperated on an art project, it would help them cooperate in other areas of their lives. It would help their community.

Sy Greben wanted to help Judy. She later explained, "The city was amazed at the work I was doing, making murals with kids who had scared directors out of neighborhood centers." Sy Greben wanted Judy to keep painting.

The Great Wall of Los Angeles *mural was painted on a flood control wall along the Tujunga Wash. The Tujunga Wash was a natural river channel of the Los Angeles river. It was turned into a concrete ditch to prevent floods like the one pictured here.*

Chapter 4:
Coming Into Her Own

The work Judy had done on her own time was rewarded. Sy Greben made Judy a paid director of a city mural program. The program included more neighborhoods in East Los Angeles. Teens were hired who had been in trouble with the police. Sy Greben thought they might stay out of trouble if they had something interesting to do.

Judy's mural program grew. In 1974, it was given a new name: the Citywide Murals Program. The program spread to neighborhoods across the city and Judy hired teens from her earlier mural crews. They helped her run the program.

As the project grew, Judy worked with hundreds of **multicultural** youth (kids of all races). They painted over 400 murals under her **supervision.** Judy learned new skills. She had to deal with people in City Hall and she had to deal with the kids.

Addressing a Problem

The Citywide Murals Program ran into a **censorship** problem its first year. People wanted murals that showed both good and bad parts of *barrio* life. But city leaders did not want murals showing people struggling with police. They told Judy to stop painting those types of murals. They said they would stop giving money to the program if Judy did not agree.

Judy did not think the city should tell people what to paint. The people were the ones who had to look at the murals in their neighborhoods. They should be the ones to decide. Other people who worked for the city agreed with Judy. They encouraged her to start her own organization. They told her it would give her more freedom. She would not have to worry about the city taking away her **funding.** She could find other sources of money.

Judy followed this advice. In 1976 she and two other women formed the Social and Public Art Resource Center, or SPARC. The other women were a filmmaker named Donna Deitch and a high school art teacher named Christina Schlesinger. SPARC supported public art. Public art is art done by people in the community. It is put where the community can see it. SPARC wanted to bring artists and people from many **ethnic** groups together.

Christina created the name SPARC (pronounced like the word *spark*). She explained, "Just as one tiny spark can become a large grass fire. One idea can start a new way of doing things." The mural movement that spread across Los Angeles had a new home.

The Tujunga Wash

SPARC began its first mural in 1976. It was called *The Great Wall of Los Angeles.* The **United States Army Corps of Engineers** hired SPARC to paint the mural in a flood control channel called the Tujunga Wash. A flood control channel is a large ditch where extra water flows during a flood. The Corps thought a mural would improve the looks of the ditch. It had once been a dirt ditch. Now, it was a wide, ugly, concrete scar. It divided the land and stretched for miles. Its walls were thirteen and a half feet high.

Judy had an idea to paint the history of Los Angeles in the Tujunga Wash. Again, she would work with the community. They would paint events that had been left out of history books. They would paint the stories of their ancestors and of people living there now. They would paint the stories of normal people.

Mexican Mural Artists

Someone gave Judy a book named *Los Tres Grandes* ("The Three Greats"). It was about three Mexican muralists named Diego Rivera, David Alfaro Siqueiros, and José Clemente Orozco. They painted murals in the first half of the 1900s. Mural painting in the United States came from their work.

The book inspired Judy to learn more. In 1977 she went to Mexico. Judy saw murals that had been painted on the walls of buildings. She saw murals on bridges and other large surfaces. Judy wanted to know more. She decided to study for a few months at the studio of David Alfaro Siqueiros.

Siqueiros was dead, but people still worked at his studio. They had learned before he died. Those people taught others. Judy took classes at the studio. She learned the best kinds of materials to use and new ways to paint. Judy came back from Mexico inspired by what she had learned. She was ready to begin work on *The Great Wall.*

David Alfaro Siqueiros (1896–1974)

Siqueiros was the artist who influenced Judy Baca the most. He fought in the Mexican Revolution during the 1910s and then studied in Spain from 1919 to 1922. After he returned to Mexico, he painted on mostly government buildings. He also became active in politics. He was jailed several times over the next 40 years for helping labor **unions** and for other political beliefs.

Siqueiros used light and shadow, a few colors, bold shapes, and large figures to create a forceful effect. He often sprayed colors from a paint gun when he decorated large buildings. His murals often show the changes in Mexican society after the Revolution, and his belief in fair treatment of the working class and the poor. He also painted small pictures. One of his best-known paintings is called *Echo of a Cry* (1937).

Diego Rivera (1886–1957)

Diego Rivera was a muralist and one of Mexico's most famous artists. He began to study art at the age of ten. He studied and lived in Europe from 1907 to 1921. In 1921 Rivera returned to Mexico after meeting David Alfaro Siqueiros. The two wanted to create a new national art inspired by the Mexican Revolution, which took place from 1910 to 1920.

This is a part of a Rivera mural in a government building in Mexico.

Rivera began painting huge murals in public buildings all over the country. In a mural for the National Palace in Mexico City, Rivera painted the history of Mexico. Rivera painted Indians, farmers, and factory workers in bright colors. His human figures were solid, simple shapes in dark, bold lines.

From 1930 to 1934, Rivera worked in the United States. He painted a mural called *Man at the Crossroads* at Rockefeller Center in New York City. It had the figure of a Russian leader, **communist** Vladimir Lenin. The people who had hired Rivera did not like it. They had the work destroyed. Rivera returned to Mexico and made a copy of the mural for the Palace of Fine Arts in Mexico City. He died in 1957 before he could finish a giant mural he was working on for the National Palace.

This section of The Great Wall of Los Angeles *shows popular musicians from the 1930s. Music from that time is a part of the history of the people who lived in the city.*

Chapter 5:
Going International

Judy began planning *The Great Wall* mural before she left for Mexico. She wanted the mural to show important events from ancient times through modern times. It would show ordinary people who had been a part of the history of Los Angeles. The mural would show dinosaurs in a tar pit. It would show Spanish explorers arriving by ship and Chinese workers building the railroad. It would show farm workers and Japanese Americans.

Work on the mural began in 1976. Judy had eighty teenagers to **supervise** the first summer. The youths were paid with money from a city summer program. After she returned from Mexico in 1977, Judy remembered what she had learned there. She used that knowledge on new parts of *The Great Wall.*

For eight summers, Judy worked with people of all ages and backgrounds. Paid workers and volunteers helped Judy with the mural. Everyone shared ideas. Over the years, Judy worked with thousands of people of all ages and **cultures.**

The Great Wall Method

Judy used a group process to plan *The Great Wall.* First, people were interviewed about their family history and their lives in Los Angeles. Judy also talked with 40 history professors.

Next, teams of artists offered their ideas. Then, groups of teenagers and adult volunteers painted the mural. They used images to tell stories of family histories. By working with others, people learned to respect their differences. Teens learned to work together to solve problems. Adults learned more about the teens they worked with. Working toward a common goal built trust among everybody. Friendships were formed that lasted for years.

Judy, third from left, with one of the painting crews that worked on The Great Wall.

Doing Other Things

Judy went back to school. She earned a master's degree in art in 1979 from California State University at Northridge. Work continued on *The Great Wall.* Judy saw that the mural could be a model for other mural projects. She would develop a program for artists.

The program was called the Muralist Training Workshop. A workshop teaches skills to people in a certain field. The workshop began to train artists in 1981. Students learned how to organize a project, and how to train volunteers and experts to work together. They learned how to develop an idea for a mural. They learned how to do research and paint murals.

More people took notice of Judy's work. In the early 1980s, Judy accepted a new teaching job at the University of California at Irvine. Every summer, she continued work on *The Great Wall.* It was completed in 1984. It was thirteen and a half feet high and a half-mile long. *The Great Wall* is thought to be the world's longest mural. It is one of Judy's greatest accomplishments.

The World Wall

After *The Great Wall* was finished, Judy thought about a question one teen had asked. "Why not make a global version of *The Great Wall?*" the teen had suggested. The question stayed with Judy.

Slowly an idea took shape. Judy would work with people from different countries. In 1987 Judy began planning a mural called *The World Wall: A Vision of the Future Without Fear.*

The new mural would not show history. Instead, it would show the future in a world without violence. Judy wanted artists from other countries to offer ideas. But there was a problem. If she involved people from other countries, where would they paint?

The Idea of Peace

Judy planned *The World Wall* to be a different kind of mural. She wanted people from other countries to see it. The mural would have to be portable. The mural would have seven panels. Each one would be 10-by-30 feet high. Judy and her team of helpers would paint some of the panels. Artists from different countries would paint other panels.

The World Wall: A Vision of the Future Without Fear *is a mural on panels that can be moved. People all over the world can see it. Judy painted the above panel. It is called* Triumph of the Hearts. *It shows how people can bring peaceful change.*

The World Wall *has sections by artists from different countries. Two Mexican artists, Martha Ramirez and Patricia Quijano, painted this section. Its name is* Tlazolteotl: Creative Force of the Un-Woven.

Starting the new project was difficult. It was hard for the teens who worked with her to imagine a world of peace. It was easier for them to imagine a world destroyed by war.

Judy thought that the first step toward world peace was to imagine it. If people could not do that, how could they ever hope for peace to happen? She did an exercise with her young assistants. She wanted to help them understand the nature of peace. Everyone gathered in a large circle and held out their hands. Judy told them that every hand in the circle was needed to make the project work.

Another Program

Judy worked on plans for *The World Wall.* In 1988 the mayor of Los Angeles asked her to develop a new city mural program. It was called Neighborhood Pride: Great Walls Unlimited Program. The goal was to paint a mural in almost every **ethnic** community in Los Angeles. It trained hundreds of artists and young people. Over many years, they created more than one hundred murals.

Painting the Idea of Peace

Judy talked to many people about her ideas for *The World Wall*. She talked about the method she had used to create her earlier mural, *The Great Wall*. She told how she wanted to use a similar process for the new mural.

Judy found artists in other countries to work on *The World Wall*. Judy exchanged information and ideas of a peaceful world with them. It took several years of planning.

The World Wall had its **premier** in Finland in 1990. The panels were arranged in a semicircle. The mural traveled to other countries. In each country the mural visited, local artists completed another panel. New panels were arranged in an outer circle. Older panels were in the inner circle.

The World Wall was displayed at the Smithsonian Museum in Washington, D.C. Then it continued its travels during the 1990s and into the 2000s. When the mural is not traveling, its permanent home is at SPARC.

Judy had planned for the mural to have seven panels. It grew to fourteen panels. She says that the number could grow in the future. It may never be completely finished. To Judy, *The World Wall* is important because of its powerful message of peace.

Social and Public Art Resource Center

SPARC was founded in 1976 by Judy Baca, Donna Deitch, and Christina Schlesinger. SPARC is dedicated to supporting artists in the creation of murals that reflect the many **ethnic** communities in Los Angeles.

Here are some of the works SPARC has sponsored over the years. Those listed below were created in the 1980s and 1990s.

The Offering by Yreina Cervantez. This work is a tribute to Latino farm workers and **union** members. A union is an organization that supports the rights of workers. The Spanish title is *La Ofrenda.*

East Meets West by Vibul Wonprasat. This work shows the contributions that Asians have brought to Los Angeles.

Not Somewhere Else, But Here by Daryl Elaine Wells. This mural appears on a wall of the building for the National Council of Jewish Women. It features famous female social activists, Jewish and otherwise.

Freedom Won't Wait by Noni Olabisi. This mural in South Los Angeles shows the violence of **racism.**

One of Judy Baca's students stands in front of his mural, Arnoldo's Brother.

Chapter 6: Branching Out

J udy taught for fifteen years at California State University at Monterey Bay. In the mid-1990s, she helped start a new school department called the Visual and Public Art Institute. Judy and the other founders turned an old military base into the new art school. They had found a peaceful use for the old base.

One day Judy received a telephone call. It was from the University of California at Los Angeles (UCLA). UCLA is one of ten schools in the University of California system. The different branches are located all over the state. UCLA wanted Judy to work for them. They explained that some students had gone on a hunger strike. In a hunger strike, people refuse to eat anything until their demands are met.

The students wanted the university to offer a program in **Chicano** studies. They wanted to learn about Mexican-American **culture.** They were willing to go hungry until they got what they wanted.

One of Judy Baca's UCLA students created this mural, called Familia ("Family" in Spanish.

The students believed the school would not listen to them unless they did something to get attention. That is why they went on the hunger strike. They wanted a Mexican American to teach them about **Chicano culture.** Judy agreed to take the job.

Judy began teaching at UCLA in 1996. She worked in two departments. The first department has a very long name. It is called the César Chávez Center for Interdisciplinary Instruction in Chicana and Chicano Studies. *Interdisciplinary* means to study a subject from many points of view.

The Chávez Center taught students about the art, history, and literature of Chicano culture. Students learned about the many achievements of Mexican Americans. Judy's art often focused on the struggles of people who suffered from poverty and **racism.** Her work inspired her students.

Judy also worked in a department at UCLA called World Arts and Cultures. She was a professor of art. She had worked with artists from other countries on *The World Wall.* That experience helped her in this new job.

The Rewards of Peace

Judy's work at UCLA was rewarded. She became one of the few **Chicana** professors in the University of California system to be offered a job with tenure. Tenure is another name for being able to keep the job in a university. Becoming a professor with tenure is a big achievement.

Judy thought back to when she was little. She thought about how her grandmother had taken care of the people around her. She had taught Judy the importance of loving one's family. She had taught Judy about healing people.

Then Judy remembered her first year of teaching. She remembered how she lost that job because she had marched for peace. She had been upset about being fired from her first teaching job. Now, she had reached the top of her profession. She had continued to work for peace. The rewards had been great.

A New Way to Make Murals

Judy was very busy with her different jobs. She taught at UCLA. She continued to work at SPARC. Judy wanted to teach more people to make murals. She looked for a way that would let more people work on them. She chose a method called **digital imaging.**

Digital imaging uses computers and digital cameras to design murals. Pictures or images taken with a digital camera can be put in a computer. Then, on the computer the artist can change a picture in many ways. It can be made much larger. It can be combined with other pictures.

Judy needed a place where students could learn this new way to make murals. She started the UCLA Digital Mural Laboratory. The laboratory holds classes at SPARC. Judy was excited about the more modern way to make murals.

Digital imaging makes it easier to preserve murals. Artists paint pictures on sheets of aluminum. Then they attach the aluminum sheets to the walls of buildings. Murals on aluminum can easily be saved. They can be removed before an old building is destroyed.

More than a Mural

With the new **technology**, Judy taught her students how to plan and paint a mural. Judy used the same process she had always used. First, her students learned the history of a place. They needed to know the importance of working with the community. They gathered ideas from people there. Then students decided what to include in a mural. They combined their ideas with those of the people they talked to.

She explained, "They are creating places of public memory. They must ask themselves, 'What should we remember? Whose story should we tell, and why?'"

Judy's students learned about the **cultures** and communities in which their murals were placed. They enjoyed creating murals with people in the community. They made new friends. They spent a lot of time with them. Some of them became as close as family.

The students wanted the people who lived there to see that their stories were worth telling. Judy and fifteen students then created six murals for the community center of Estrada Courts. It is one of the oldest housing projects in East Los Angeles. A housing project offers housing for people with low incomes.

Each mural tells something about the people who live there. Some murals are about their roots. Some show the things that are important in their lives. One student remembered how different creating the murals was from other learning experiences. "What we learned went beyond art. We learned to work together creatively," the student said.

Preserving a National Treasure:
America Tropical by David Alfaro Siqueiros

Sometimes murals are destroyed because people do not agree with their subject. In 1932 Mexican mural artist David Alfaro Siqueiros painted an 80-foot-tall mural in Los Angeles. People expected Siqueiros to paint a happy Mexican village scene. He did not. His mural called *America Tropical* showed in symbols how poorly Mexican workers in California were treated. A symbol is something that stands for something else. People were shocked by Siqueiros's mural. The city had the mural painted over with white paint.

Towards the end of the 1900s, the city decided the mural should be saved. It was the only public mural by Siqueiros left in the United States. The mural was cleaned and given a protective coating, then opened to the public in the early 2000s. Judy's students made a mural for an exhibit scheduled with the opening. An exhibit shows many paintings or works of art. The mural Judy's group made was called *Los Angeles Tropical.* They used **digital imaging** to put a part of Siqueiros' mural in the middle of theirs. The students' mural shows historic scenes of poverty and hardship.

Because many murals are outside where they are exposed to the weather, they must be maintained. Here a Los Angeles artist checks the surface of his 21-year-old mural.

Chapter 7: Meaningful Work

Murals do not last unless they are taken care of. They are damaged when a building is destroyed. They are damaged when people paint **graffiti** on them. Pollution, weather, and neglect can ruin outdoor murals. By the year 2000, sunlight and rain had faded *The Great Wall* mural. Each year, floodwaters poured into the Tujunga Wash. Each time, the water damaged the mural a little more.

Only a few murals are protected by the government. Usually, artists must take care of the murals they paint. Judy worked with the Social and Public Art Resource Center (SPARC) to raise money to repaint *The Great Wall.* It would cost more than a million dollars to restore the mural.

Judy explained that it was worth the cost. "The people who have worked on this project gave much more than their time," she said. They made something worth keeping. They made a giant memorial to peace between the races.

More Work on the Mural

The Great Wall was begun in 1976. The year 2001 marked its 25th anniversary. Judy knew that many people who had worked on the mural still lived nearby. She asked them to help restore it.

One woman named Ernestine had worked on *The Great Wall* when she was fourteen. She had been in a lot of trouble. Judy worked closely with the troubled girl. She had brought people to talk with Ernestine and the other teens.

One person was a Holocaust survivor who had survived the German death camps during World War II. The Holocaust was the killing of millions of people simply because they were Jews or members of other **ethnic** groups.

Ernestine remembered that visit for a long time. She began to realize that her problems were small compared to those of others. Ernestine worked on the mural for six years. She became a crew leader. She told how the work helped her. "It saved my life," she said.

Mark Meisels worked on the mural as a teenager. The experience gave him direction in life. It helped him choose a career. He became an assistant set decorator for movies. A set decorator gathers materials to create backgrounds for movie scenes. He said the mural was the reason he got into the movie business.

Mark heard that Judy was calling for people to help restore the mural. He said, "I would like to be part of that again, even if it is only for a day."

Judy wanted to do more than restore *The Great Wall.* She wanted to add more about the history of Los Angeles. She wanted to paint more stories that were important to local people.

Judy's art students helped her plan. The events on the original mural ended with the 1950s. Judy's students studied what had happened since then. They learned about events that took place between the 1960s and the 1990s. They talked to people who had lived in the community during those years. They planned for the *The Great Wall* to show some of these stories.

Being Recognized

Judy has been honored for her work. In 2001 the National Hispanic Heritage Foundation gave Judy an award in Washington, D.C. for her teaching.

That same year, Judy was the guest of First Lady Laura Bush at a luncheon honoring First Lady Marta Fox of Mexico. *First Lady* is the title given to the wife of a president. Judy was chosen to be a guest because she represents the Mexican-American community.

Judy is now in her late 50s. She still teaches at the University of California at Los Angeles. She continues her work at SPARC. She constantly works on new mural projects that bring to life the experiences of many people. She speaks to many groups about the important work she and others at SPARC are doing.

A list of the work that Judy has done cannot begin to tell her whole story. Judy uses art to bring people of all ages and backgrounds together. She has taught thousands of people about the value of having a purpose in life. Judy's way of using art to give a voice to ordinary people continues to impact many communities.

Some Judy Baca Works, from 1990s through Early 2000s

This is a section of La Memoria de Nuestra Tierra: Colorado.

La Memoria de Nuestra Tierra: Colorado (Our Land Has Memory) 1999

This 50-foot digital mural at the Denver International Airport shows the history of the Denver area and its people. For Judy, the project was a personal one. Her grandparents settled in Colorado after leaving Mexico.

Durango Mural Project 2001

Judy worked with Southern Ute Indians and **Chicano** youth in Durango, Colorado. They used **digital imaging** to build the mural over the Internet. The 20-foot by 35-foot work was produced on tiles that were placed on the exterior of the city's Fine Arts Center.

Fifteen Digital Tile Murals on the Boardwalk at Venice Beach, California 2002

These tiles offer a self-guided tour to historic Venice murals reproduced on tiles. Venice is a suburb of Los Angeles. SPARC is located there.

Glossary

abstract does not have a direct relation to the real world. Abstract art does not look like a real object or picture.

barrio Spanish-speaking neighborhood in a city or town

censorship leaving out something that people object to

Chicano/a Mexican American

civil war war between people who live in the same country

communism system of government in which everything is owned by the government

culture values, beliefs, and way of life shared by a group of people

digital imaging use of computers, software, digital cameras, and scanners to create an image

discrimination unfair treatment of a group of people based on their race or other characteristic

ethnic large group of people that have a similar background based on common things such as race, religion, language, or nationality

funding money given to a person or organization to pay for a project

graffiti drawing or writing on a public surface such as a wall

landlord owner of an apartment or house that is rented to another person

lookout person assigned to warn others of approaching danger

multicultural reflecting or representing many cultures

prehistoric time before history was written down

premier display or show something for the first time

racism belief that one race of people is better than another

republican government in which people choose their leaders

scaffold platform that allows painters to work at a height above the floor or ground

supervise oversee or watch over people

technology specialized method or tool

union organization of workers

unite bring together

United States Army Corps of Engineers government organization that builds and maintains roads and dams

Timeline

1946: Judy Baca is born in Los Angeles, California.

1964: Enrolls at the University of California in Northridge.

1969: Graduates from college. Begins teaching at her former high school; works with students on her first cooperative art project.

1970: Begins teaching art for the City of Los Angeles. Paints murals with gang members.

1974: Begins the Citywide Murals Project.

1976: Co-founds the Social and Public Art Resource Center (SPARC). Begins *The Great Wall,* the world's longest mural.

1977: Studies mural art in Mexico.

1981: Develops Muralist Training Program at SPARC.

1987: Begins work on *The World Wall: A Vision of the Future Without Fear.*

1988: Develops a new mural program for the city of Los Angeles called Great Walls Unlimited: Neighborhood Pride Program.

1990: Completes four of the seven panels of *The World Wall* and travels to the former Soviet Union and Finland to display the work-in-progress.

1996: Begins teaching at the University of California at Los Angeles. Begins experimenting with digital imaging to make murals.

2000: Completes mural for the Denver International Airport.

2001: Begins restoring *The Great Wall* for the 25th anniversary of the mural. Begins updating the mural with events through the 1990s. Receives Hispanic Heritage Foundation award for her teaching.

Further Information

Further reading

Ancona, George. *Murals: Walls that Sing.* New York: Marshall
  Cavendish, 2003.

Cruz, Bárbara. *José Clemente Orozco: Mexican Artist.* Springfield, NJ:
  Enslow Publishers, 1998.

Fernández, Mayra. *Judy Baca: Artist.* Cleveland, OH: Modern Curriculum
  Press, 1994.

Addresses

SPARC
(Social and Public
Art Resource Center)
685 Venice Boulevard
Venice, CA 90291

César Chávez Center
for Interdisciplinary Instruction
in Chicana and Chicano Studies
UCLA
Bunche Hall 7349
Mailcode 155 903
Los Angeles, CA 90095-1559

Index

FREE PUBLIC LIBRARY UNION, NEW JERSEY

3 9549 00392 6996